W. Victor Maloy

NIGHT MUSINGS

A Collection of
Spiritual Vignettes of Life

Published by the Virginia Institute of Pastoral Care, Inc.,
2000 Bremo Road, Suite 105, Richmond, VA 23226 (804) 282-8332

Printed by The Business Press, Richmond, VA 23230

i

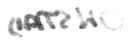

ISBN: 0-9717869-0-9

TABLE OF CONTENTS

FOREWORD

Vic Maloy is our friend and a gifted writer with great sensitivity.

He writes a column called "Night Musings" that is a "must read" in InTouch, the newsletter of the Virginia Institute of Pastoral Care. The columns are about his personal experiences and are written with such intimacy that the reader can't help but feel that he or she is part of the experiences.

We thought a book of his columns would be a good way to recognize this fine writer as he prepares to take office for a two-year term as president of the American Association of Pastoral Counselors while continuing to serve as VIPCare's executive director. We prevailed upon Vic to let us help get the book published. We hope you will enjoy reading it as much as we have enjoyed helping put it together.

George Crutchfield
Alf Goodykoontz

January 2002

ACKNOWLEDGEMENTS

Without the invitation of Donald D. Denton, the editor of the newsletter of the Virginia Institute of Pastoral Care, these pieces would not have been written. I am grateful for his persistence in encouraging me to write a regular column for the newsletter and for the freedom to write about whatever was stirring in my soul when the deadline arrived!

There are those of you who read these columns and took the time to tell me that they touched deep places in your heart and should be more widely circulated. Your words have encouraged me to continue to make my private musings public.

To Alf Goodykoontz and George Crutchfield of the board of directors of the Virginia Institute of Pastoral Care, I am grateful for making the publication of these columns possible. I have been touched at every turn by their interest in and desire to see these articles published. Their professional editorial expertise and sense of humor have made this venture a delightful experience! In taking my writing so seriously they have helped me to better understand writing as an expression of ministry.

The manuscript was typed by Barbara King, who for many years was the administrative assistant at the Virginia Institute of Pastoral Care. I am grateful now as then for her careful attention to detail and her unerring ability to decipher my handwriting!

The recent invitations from Eastern Mennonite Seminary and the Atlantic Region of the American

Association of Pastoral Counselors to read some of these stories in a worship context have been most helpful. Presenting them orally has provided an opportunity to see that the stories are meant for the ear as well as the eye.

My wife Susan suggested the titles for each of the vignettes. You will see in the titles a glimpse of the depth of the sensitivity of her soul, without which my soul and these stories would be greatly diminished.

INTRODUCTION

Most of my boyhood summers were spent with my grandparents on the Eastern Shore of Virginia in a very small town named Bloxom. A railroad track bisected the town, and I remember about four stores on each side of the tracks. The stores were where the locals socialized as much as they did business. An early memory is of being sent to the store for some very sharp cheddar cheese and upon entering the store noticing that silence had replaced the loud voices and laughter as I walked through the door. Only when I announced to the shopkeeper that I was Carson Barnes' grandson did the talking and laughter resume! Such was the close-knit quality of the community. It was decades later before I heard the term "come heres" – and never once did I think of myself as one!

It was in that hot and humid summer setting, where time seemed endless, that I learned to catch fireflies and play mumble peg and shoot marbles. It was also where I came to love stories.

Dinner around my grandparents' table was an event! Long before dinnertime, the kitchen filled with the wonderful smells of my grandmother's cooking. Dinner around the large oak table was accompanied by long conversations and stories about people and events in the community that were funny and at times poignant and sad. My grandfather was a consummate storyteller. Puffing on his after-dinner pipe, he would tell wonderful and mostly true stories! It was in that setting, summer after summer, that I was nourished by stories, came to understand the importance of stories, and learned to listen and look for stories.

The stories gathered here are like the stories that I heard all those years ago. Some are funny and others poignant and sad. All come from moments in my life. Some have been painful to write and I have wept while writing some of them. Others have been joyous to write and I have laughed out loud while writing them!

I have tried to tell each story as simply as possible, and how I felt as it happened. Even though I am trained as a minister to reflect on life from a theological and spiritual perspective, I have left the meaning of each story to the reader. I trust that each reader will find his or her own story within these stories.

Our wonderful poet laureate, Stanley Kunitz, has written:

> *In my darkest night,*
> *when the moon*
> *was covered*
> *and I roamed through*
> *wreckage,*
> *a nimbus-clouded voice*
> *directed me:*
> *"Live in tbe layers,*
> *not on the litter."*

The stories that follow are moments of life lived in the layers.

MATURING AND RETIRING

This has been a summer of head-turning transition in my life. One of the lights of my life, my daughter Kristin, has graduated from high school and now begins a more grown-up phase of her life. A few months ago I escorted her onto the football field to stand with the candidates for homecoming queen. Standing there, I began to realize that the end of a certain precious phase of our relationship was occurring. With immense love, I stood there in the Florida sun with her arm through mine. With pride, I stood by myself as she went forward to receive the flowers and crown and the traditional ride in the convertible. As the pictures were taken and she chatted excitedly with her boyfriend, I stood on the periphery of the crowd feeling the edge of my sadness, realizing that the centrality of my role in her life was coming to an end.

We would, of course, continue to cherish each other, but I was now becoming less central in her life and appropriately so, as her life moved to take in other people and events. The lump in my throat as I stood there was out of deep gratitude for our closeness through the years and grief at the natural ending of an irreplaceable time between us. More recently, my wife and I stood watching Kristin as she walked down the airport corridor toward her plane. As she disappeared into the crowd, my wife's poignant words were "Well, she's gone." Not of course in any final sense, but in the sense that our relationship is changing and we must now struggle to see what new forms it takes.

As the other end of the continuum, another of the

lights of my life, my uncle, retired this summer after many years as a college administrator. Carson was an early important male role model in my development. He taught me to drive one summer on the Eastern Shore of Virginia when I was 10 years old. It was a black 1934 V8 Ford. He said, and I have no reason to doubt, that it would run 85 miles an hour. He simply announced that if we were going to get back home, I would have to do the driving. I did and we did and much of my life since has been governed by that admonition.

He taught me how to stand up to the neighborhood bully by threatening to punish me if I let the bully beat me up again. I had no trouble with the bully after that. He sat long hours at the kitchen table with me when I did not want to do my math homework in elementary school. He sent me a baseball glove when I was in high school and encouraged me to play sports, giving me pointers. He wrote me a loving letter of encouragement when I was in the hospital my senior year of high school and could not finish the football season.

But beyond all of those significant gestures, he was a steady presence and example that I could go to college, that I could find a profession, that I could make a contribution. Without his influence, I suspect my life would have turned in directions vastly different and more limited. So while I rejoice for Carson in his retirement, it is difficult for me no longer to think of his steady presence out there on the college campus. In an odd way, it leaves me feeling a little less secure about life. A familiar landmark has changed as with my daughter.

A BALCONY OF MEMORY

I have no idea why the past sometimes appears suddenly in the present, unbidden by any conscious thought. Perhaps an errant neuron fired by the brain. Perhaps some hunger of the heart seeking resolution. Whichever, it came suddenly and unbidden as I stood on the hotel balcony, mesmerized by the neon-lit skyline of Dallas. Earlier in the day I had chanced to see a line in the window of a store, "Any sufficiently advanced technology is indistinguishable from magic." Later that evening, standing on the balcony with the neon skyline etched against the sky and thinking about that line, I remembered Joe Johnson.

I had gone to Dallas in an attempt to live out a belief that I had uttered in other places. That second choices in life often turn out to be better for us than our first choices. That much of life has to do with learning to accommodate and adapt when we do not get what we want. That the mark of health and wholeness and holiness has to do with adaptation. It was in that spirit that I made my way to Dallas.

My alma mater had spent September and October undefeated and overwhelmingly ranked as the number one college football team in the country. I had already begun to make plans to see them win the national title in the Orange Bowl, when in three devastating weeks in November they lost their final two games of the season and were eliminated from consideration. The Cotton Bowl hardly seemed a consolation for not getting my first choice. I was mean-spirited in my disappointment, and as a result, the Cotton Bowl was ready to be played before I made my contrite way to Dallas.

I do not know if I would have ever thought about Joe Johnson if I had gone to the Orange Bowl and gazed upon the Miami skyline. So much of life seems dictated by circumstance. I had not thought about Joe in 30 years. Not since the beginning of my junior year of high school. Yet there in Dallas on New Year's night came the memory.

Joe Johnson hanged himself in the summer of 1960 between our sophomore and junior years of high school. I did not know Joe and found out on the first day of school when the principal made the terse announcement over the P.A. system and asked for a moment of silence. The announcement was that Joe had died. Only later did I learn he had hanged himself. No one seemed to know why or to have anticipated it.

There in Dallas on the hotel balcony I tried to remember what Joe looked like. I could not even remember his name that evening. Only that a classmate of mine had killed himself and I needed to know more about him.

When I returned home I found my high school yearbook. Inside was an "In Memoriam" page and picture of Joe. I remembered seeing him in the hallways, but I have no memory of ever having spoken to him or he to me. In the yearbook Joe's eyes look shy and sad and empty. It is hard to know how much of that is my own sadness for Joe or for me. Sitting with his picture and my tears, I wished for a memory of having spoken to him.

Instead, I found my way to Dallas and to that balcony and to the memory of Joe Johnson and the opportunity, 30 years later, to weep for his loss and mine.

A COLLAR, A BANDANNA, A GOODBYE

October, with all of its beauty, has broken my heart. I had been in the West Virginia mountains for two days on business. It was the most glorious fall I could remember. The leaves were at their peak and the sky so blue and cloudless that it hardly seemed real. I had been mostly indoors and busy with committee work when I took a break to return a call from my wife. Our aging 14-year-old German Shepherd, Spike, had been ill for several weeks and we had been awaiting his test results. My wife's words were flat and measured, "The vet says it is terminal and he will try and keep Spike going until you get home in two days. I made an appointment to put him to sleep at 3:30 on Sunday." Standing in the hallway at the pay phone, tears began to run down my face and I heard my voice as if coming from a great distance, "If I can work it out, I will try and drive back tonight. I will let you know."

It was as if I could not breathe inside the building. Blinking back my tears, I tried to avoid my colleagues and made my way outside and down to the lake. There by the lake and alone, I sobbed. I remember kicking the ground and saying, "No, not on such a beautiful day!" Standing there, I remembered saying to students and colleagues that what I had learned about being with people, I had learned from lying on the floor with my nose against Spike's and staring into his eyes. There was no question in my mind at that moment that my professional responsibilities were not as important as my relationship to Spike. I composed myself and went back to

5

my committee to make arrangements to leave for home that night.

I felt numb as I moved among my colleagues. I waited until the end of our meeting that afternoon before telling them, afraid of the intensity of my feelings. They were kind and sympathetic and quick to take care of my responsibilities for the following day. After everyone had left and I was gathering up my paperwork, one of my colleagues stood in front of me and said, "I am sorry." My eyes filled with tears and I could only nod a recognition. She reached out and hugged me tenderly, and her hug carried me along the long, lonely drive back to Richmond. The drive in the darkness was strangely comforting. I felt insulated and protected from the coming loss and a sense that time was suspended. I arrived home just before midnight and went straight into the den where I knew I would find him. There Spike lay on his side too weak to get up. When he saw me he weakly wagged his tail. I bent down, kissed him on his nose, and said, "Hi, sweetie."

So intent was I on getting home that I had not called my wife to let her know I was coming. Spike had grown steadily weaker after our phone conversation and Susan thought he would not live through the night. In desperation she told me that she sat on the floor with him and said again and again, "Just hold on. He will be here soon." Until the wee hours of the next morning, we sat on the floor with Spike, stroking him and crying. When the need for sleep finally overtook us, Spike was too weak to climb the stairs to our bedroom, so we put him on a sheet and carried him upstairs. Not wanting him to die alone, I found my sleeping bag and slept on the floor beside him.

Spike had not eaten in a week and I fully expected

him to die as we slept. Instead, when I awoke beside him on the floor the next morning, he was staring at me, waiting for me to wake up. My coming home seemed to have rejuvenated him. He walked down the stairs and by the afternoon was eating a sandwich from Arby's. The three of us spent that Saturday on the patio — a beautiful day filled with hope and denial. Neither of us spoke of the next day's 3:30 appointment. Finally, late in the day as twilight was approaching, Susan said softly, "This lovely day is coming to an end and it will never be again." Her words touched a level of grief I had not experienced before. I sobbed uncontrollably and I am sure for everything I had ever lost in my life. I said to Susan that I knew how to accept Spike's death, but that I did not know how to take his life from him when he was in no obvious pain. Finally, in darkness on the patio, we agreed that the three of us would know when the time to let go had come.

We did keep the 3:30 appointment the next day, but only so that the vet could assure us that Spike was in no pain. He said simply, "It looks like he isn't ready to leave you just yet." And he wasn't. But his appetite was slowly slipping away again and we realized that the day before had been a gift — a moment of reprieve from the inevitable.

What shall I say of that last week with Spike? There were exquisite moments in the midst of our grief. Each night we carried him on his sheet up to our bedroom, where I continued to sleep on the floor with him. We came home from work during the day and brought him Arby's sandwiches, trying to stimulate his appetite. Our hearts broke as this dog, who so loved to eat, could eat no longer. Together, the three of us had two beautiful weekends on the patio, filled with such sweetness and purity of presence that I thought my heart would break into pieces.

On that final Sunday, Spike let us know that he was ready. As we sat on the patio, he seemed increasingly disoriented and uncharacteristically moved farther and farther away from us. Finally, he lay in the leaves under the bushes and stared off into the distance as though he saw and heard something that we did not. We realized that he was trying to leave us and that our grief was making it difficult.

The next day was Halloween. When I came through the door at 7:30 that evening and saw Susan sitting on the sofa, I knew. That morning Susan had left our vet's phone number on my desk. I understood what she meant and called him during the day to ask if there was a more private way than for the three of us to have to sit in a noisy waiting room without dignity. Our vet understood and he said, "Of course, come after office hours."

Spike sat all Halloween evening at our front door and watched the children as they came for candy. Several of them petted him and he even managed a weak bark or two. Sitting on the sofa looking at Spike lying beside the candy dish, Susan said, "Look at him. He is starving and staying alive because he doesn't want to disappoint us. He is the one with all the courage. We now have to find enough courage of our own to help him leave." With that I went to the phone and told our vet we would be there by 8:15.

As we prepared to leave, Susan said, "Is there anything of his you would like to take?" I said, "Yes, his sheet that we carried him upstairs in." Susan straightened his red bandanna around his neck and I hooked his leash to his collar. It was such a bittersweet moment. His leash meant he was going somewhere and that always made him happy. We helped him into the car and drove the next five minutes in silence, trying to disconnect.

Spike walked peacefully into the examining room. Susan spread his sheet on the floor and Spike with almost no coaxing lay down. He seemed almost relieved. I knelt on the floor with one hand stroking his back and the other his head. The vet's assistant, a young woman, knelt on the other side and gently stroked Spike's head. Occasionally our fingers touched and it seemed an odd intimacy. I watched the vet's hands as he slowly began the injection. I wanted Spike's last awareness to be familiar and as the injection began I stroked his head and said, "Good night sweet prince, and flights of angels sing thee to thy rest." And with that a low groan escaped Spike's body and he was still. No one moved as my tears dripped steadily on to his fur. In the silence I became aware of a most beautiful thing. The vet's assistant was silently crying and her tears were gently falling on to Spike's fur and mingling with mine. It was a strangely healing moment to share such grief with someone I did not know.

Our vet and assistant left us alone with Spike to say a loving goodbye. Susan removed his collar and bandanna. We stroked him and kissed him and thanked him for being such a good dog. We stood in the hallway with our vet, not wanting to leave. He told us of putting his own dog to sleep. As he did, tears filled his eyes and his fingers moved to his trembling lips. "It never gets any easier, you know," he said. As we turned to leave, I felt sad for him, leaving him alone with Spike. We walked silently to the car, neither of us wanting to go home. We drove around in the darkness for a long time until we found the courage to face our home without Spike.

The next morning sitting at my desk I wrote to colleagues and friends, 'To those of you who have been so loving — our old companion drew his last breath at 8:30, All Saints Eve, surrounded by love and lying on his favorite sheet." And then I added for those who knew that Spike was terrified of thunder, "This morning at 8:11 as if in a final gesture, distant thunder slightly shook our empty bedroom."

The days after Spike's death were empty beyond belief. We missed the sound of his collar. We missed seeing him in the window when we left and came home. We thought we saw him out of the corner of our eye at various places in the house. Putting away his food and water dishes was painful, as was being in the grocery store and seeing dog food. We awoke repeatedly in the pre-dawn hours as if expecting something. C. S. Lewis's words spoke our experience, "No one ever told me that grief felt so like fear. There is a sort of invisible blanket between the world and me." And in a note from Susan as she struggled with her grief: "We are all fated to part. Slipping into memory."

We coped as best we could and looked for signs. Two days after Spike's death we went through all of our pictures and found several dozen wonderful pictures taken during our 14 years together. It was a most healing evening of tears and remembering. And on the third day an amazing sight. Our Christmas cactus, which had never bloomed in the seven years we had it, issued forth one single spectacular white flower.

There was yet another exquisite moment. We made the decision to have Spike cremated and his ashes returned to us. We found ourselves increasingly impatient with the nearly two-week wait. Finally, his ashes arrived and we went uneasily to pick them up, unsure of what our reaction would be. We brought them home and cautiously took them out of the box and held them. We were surprised by our reaction. We felt comforted and relieved. It was as if Spike was back with us in a different reality and his grief and ours reduced. That Monday evening, exactly two weeks after Halloween, we took Spike's ashes into his favorite room, our den. There we welcomed him home and placed his ashes in a walnut urn, a loving gift from a friend. We placed Spike's red bandanna in the urn and we remembered Tagore's gentle reflection:

> "The water in a vessel is sparkling; the water in the sea is dark. The small truth has words that are clear; the great truth has great silence."

ERASING BARRIERS

I once had a dog that loved popcorn! Late on Saturday nights while watching video movies, I would throw Spike piece after piece of popcorn. So amazing was his eye-to-mouth coordination that he rarely missed, no matter how erratic my throw.

Spike and I came to love one another late. For years I attempted to exert my will over him, but to no avail. He repeatedly ate his doghouses and escaped into the neighborhood. On one occasion, after being missing in action for several days, we found that he had taken up residence and was accepting handouts at the back door of the local middle school cafeteria. He was stubborn, but he was discerning!

Then one summer Spike developed a terrible fear of thunder. At the first sound of thunder, he would dig beneath the fence and escape the yard looking for a safer place. It was a long thunderstorm-filled summer as repeatedly we went looking for him and repeatedly filled the holes beneath the fence. In desperation I began to fill the holes with concrete blocks, stopping weekly at the hardware store for a fresh supply. But Spike was not only tenacious, he was strong. He dug up the concrete blocks as fast as I could put them down, often bloodying his paws in the process. Thus were we engaged in a struggle of wills that long, wet summer. A struggle I was destined to lose, thankfully.

It is awesome to me how a seemingly simple

moment of life can transform and forever change the direction of a life or relationship. Late that summer, after yet another thunderstorm, I arrived home just as it was getting dark and just in time to see Spike digging beneath the fence again. It was pouring rain as I ran to the fence, pulled Spike back and began to put more concrete blocks in the hole. The water was running down my back and into my eyes when I gradually became aware that Spike was standing beside me, watching with a kind of detached curiosity. For a very long moment there in the rain, we stared into each other's eyes. Something profound and inexplicable occurred between us that I only understood years later. All I recognized in the moment was that I was defeated.

I put down the concrete block I was holding and never picked up another. Spike and I went into the house together, two very wet souls. From that point on I began to learn how to cooperate instead of continuing to engage in a struggle of wills. Spike became an indoor dog for the first time in his life. It was what he had wanted all along! He became loving and cooperative and with all the popcorn to be caught he never ran away again. The unspoken agreement that he and I reached that night in the rain transformed Spike and eventually me.

Years later when Spike was dying and not able to eat, I would bring him chicken cordon bleu sandwiches from Arby's. The last week of his life I slept beside him on the floor. Several times in the middle of the night I laid my hand on his side and thanked him for the lesson he taught me that summer of our discontent. The night that he took his final breath my last words to him were from a long ago time and place, "Goodnight sweet prince and flights of angels sing thee to thy rest."

Loren Eiseley said, "I love all the species different from my own and regret the barriers between us." I am forever grateful to Spike for the barriers he erased in my life.

FRENCH FRIES WITH CAJUN

As we drove down the road together my mother asked, "What exactly did it mean in the last newsletter that you were taking a sabbatical from the columns that you write?" I said, "Well, when the deadline came I was in the middle of two difficult trips and facing several other deadlines and I just could not find the time and energy to get the column written in time." She said "Oh" and we drove on without my telling her the real reason. It was true about the trip and the other deadlines. But the real reason I had no energy for the column was that I was dealing with the news that one of our retired racing greyhounds had been diagnosed with a terminal illness.

The call had come over dinner in Tallahassee. "The vet says that it is stage five lymphoma. Perhaps a month. Palliative care..." I do not remember the rest of the evening, other than waking up in the middle of the night crying and praying for a white light to surround Cajun. The next morning during my jog I became aware that out of the edge of my consciousness like a thin sliver of light was the feeling that if Cajun could not go on, I was not sure that I wanted to go on either. I was startled that my reaction was so intense and my connection so deep.

Cajun was our first greyhound and has been followed by three others! We first saw him from a distance six years ago. As we pulled into the parking lot where we were to pick him up, we saw a thin, classically built, jet black greyhound being walked on a leash. He had a white mark on his chest and a splash of white on his rear paws and tail. He was as graceful and elegant a creature as I have ever seen. My wife said, "Do you think he is ours?" Moments later we discovered that he was.

Our adoption of Cajun that day began a five-year journey into the world of promoting the adoption of retired racing greyhounds. Everything we learned about greyhounds, Cajun taught us. He was a reserved but wonderful ambassador as my wife took him into dozens of homes so that people interested in adopting a greyhound could meet a greyhound in person. Most asked if they could have Cajun! That probably had to do with the way in which he would curl up at the feet of people he had never met before and go to sleep! He was also a wonderful host to more than a hundred other greyhounds who passed through our home in those five years as we made a transition from the race track into an adopted home. He was forever tolerant and gracious.

I was filled with those memories as I returned home to be with Cajun after hearing the news of his illness. It was obvious that he was not feeling well and that he had begun to withdraw as animals often do when facing death. I went for a long walk alone and wept as I thought about asking Cajun to remember me. When I returned to the house, my wife said to me, "It is not helpful for Cajun to see us so sad. He needs our strength to draw from." I understood her truth. My grief was for me and my loss and to that end it was selfish. Cajun did not need me to withdraw into my own grief.

Our deeply sensitive vet placed Cajun on a medication to make him more comfortable and said he would come to our home when the time came for Cajun to leave us. I decided that my version of palliative care would be to take Cajun for a walk every morning before work and at night when I got home. And that I would take him regularly for one of his favorite foods, McDonald's french fries!

Between the medication, the walks and the french fries, Cajun is now two months past when we expected to have to let him go. As I write this, he is lying on the floor in the room with me, I suspect waiting for his next walk or trip to McDonald's! We are not under any illusion about his health. The signs are all there that the end is nearer than it was. He is weaker and his breathing more labored. But in his decision to stay a while longer, he has given us a gorgeous gift. It is the opportunity to be reminded, as I heard 83-year-old Claude Evans say, "that the prospect of death makes life shine." That when we are mindful of our limited time, the time that we do have becomes precious.

I do not pass Cajun now without stopping to touch or kiss him. With tears recently, my wife thanked me for making him an only dog for this ending time. And this always-reserved dog has decided that part of his palliative care should be to go to sleep between us in the bed. He seems to have understood what we needed and it has become a comforting ritual for him and for us.

Once in an aquarium in Vancouver I saw a quote from Loren Eiseley, "I love all the species different from my own and regret the barriers between us." Thanks to Cajun, we have been able to cross many of those barriers. The other evening I heard Garrison Keillor say, "The more that is taken away, the more precious is that which remains." That beautiful line has captured for me the meaning of these precious days with this gracious visitor.

PRECIOUS GRIEF

On the last morning of his life, E. F. Cajun Jet, our retired racing greyhound, insisted on a final walk down our steep driveway to do his duty! I should not have been surprised that this disciplined athlete should greet his death in the same courageously stoic yet gentle manner that had governed his life.

At 7 a.m. with faltering steps and in pain and panting, Cajun made his way down the driveway and across the street to the edge of the woods. When we turned to go back up, the driveway looked like Mt. Everest and I said to Cajun that I would carry him back to the house. Instead, he began to slowly walk back up the hill with a kind of determined resignation for what lay ahead. Inside the house I picked him up and carried him into our bedroom and laid him on the floor on his favorite blanket.

Cajun had so outlived his original prognosis in October that I suppose I had begun to believe that he really would live forever on a diet of McDonald's french fries and twice-a-day walks! Somewhere during those 200 walks between October and February I gave myself away and came to believe that as long as we kept walking that Cajun would keep going. A bargain, in retrospect, that I had attempted to strike with God. But now, on Valentine's Day, I was face to face with the reality that there would be no more walks and no more bargaining. We were, instead, at the end of this wondrous love affair that had crossed the barrier between species.

Our vet graciously offered to come to our house

when the moment arrived. Because he could not come until evening we had the entire day with Cajun, to remember. And there were many poignant moments to remember. There was the late fall afternoon when suddenly a gust of wind blew leaves past us on one of our walks and the old instinct kicked in and Cajun began to race the leaves! There was the Sunday evening with Cajun lying in the bed between my wife and me with his head on her shoulder. Rubbing Cajun's head Susan said, "No heroics, we will be together again." And then to no one in particular she said, "These previous moments are for the loneliness to come." And there was the couple that had lost one of their greyhounds and their embarrassment at still grieving. To which Susan's quiet response was, "Grief is precious." And so it is, I thought, as we moved through that Valentine's Day.

We scheduled workers to be at the house that morning to make indoor repairs. When they realized Cajun was dying, they offered to come back another day. Touched by their sensitivity, we nonetheless told them to stay and do the work. It was a reminder that life goes on alongside death and it was a distraction from the unrelenting movement toward evening. Cajun, always a keen observer, struggled up from the bedroom and came into the living room and lay down to watch them work!

Cajun refused all food and drink and our vet told us that would be a sign. Late in the day Cajun was still in the living room panting heavily and I knew he must be thirsty. I tried water once again and he refused. I then remembered how much he loved wine! I sat down on the floor beside him with a bowl of wine and held it while he drank every drop of it and then a second bowl! He grew quiet, stopped panting and fell asleep for the first time that day. It was a final sacrament between us.

Later, toward dusk I chanced upon a final sacrament between my wife and Cajun that was so beautifully private and tender that I turned away. As I came around the corner of the living room, Susan was sitting on the floor with a basin, gently bathing Cajun with a washcloth. As a little girl, she had read that the ancient Greeks washed the bodies of their greatest fallen warriors and covered them with rose petals.

Toward evening we received a call from our vet telling us of car trouble. We concluded that perhaps Cajun wasn't meant to die at home. We brought our other two greyhounds over to Cajun to say goodbye. In an ancient expression they each sniffed him and then I carried Cajun to the car and put him in the back seat with Susan and we made the silent hour's drive to our vet's office.

The final moments were startlingly quick. I laid Cajun on his favorite blanket and then I lay down on the floor beside him slipping my arm beneath his head as my tears dripped on his neck. Susan knelt on his other side. Cajun grew peaceful and the vet's voice was soothing. As the vet started the injection, Cajun took a deep breath, lifted his head and looked back longingly into Susan's eyes. He then sighed and slowly laid his head down in the crook of my arm. In an instant he was gone from us as mysteriously as he had come into our lives. The vet quietly left us alone in the room. There at 9 o'clock on Valentine's night, Susan reached in her purse and took out rose petals from roses that I had given her a month before on our anniversary and in the sanctity of the moment placed the rose petals on dear Cajun's body.

In the weeks that followed, I was reminded of how much grief feels like fear. A friend wrote to say that if heaven is what it is cracked up to be, Cajun will be there waiting for us. And Cajun visited Susan in successive dreams, happier each time!

Shortly before Cajun's death, I was at a banquet table with a group of people, one of whom was talking about his struggle to have another dog because of his grief over the loss of his beloved dog. He said that his heart was still broken. Almost as if I was hearing someone else speak, I heard myself say, "Our hearts are made to be broken." And so they are. As someone else once wrote, "Between grief and nothing, I will take grief."

In that sense then, my grief for Cajun is okay. It is precious grief. It allows the thinness of Cajun's very dear image to remain and last.

ARIZONA REDEMPTION

It was strange to stand there in the hot Arizona sun with tears running down my face. The warm and too greasy taco had begun to soak through the napkin the old wrinkled Indian couple had wrapped it in. I was hungry, yet the food stuck in my throat.

I had come all those miles to converse with colleagues about how to better administer pastoral counseling centers. But in search of more substantial food, I had wandered away from my hotel into the desert to the Saint Xavier Mission. I had been once before, but at a time in my life when I was less willing to allow the surroundings to speak to me. This time I had driven south from Tucson to the mission, ostensibly to find and buy a rosary, but really to find more.

The mission sat just off the interstate on an Indian reservation. Dust, short brown bushes and an absence of grass and green trees surround it. The land looked dry and stingy. Small concrete houses with no yards populated the reservation. Children and skinny dogs played in the dust and few adults were seen, only old and dusty pickup trucks. Saint Xavier Mission stood in the midst of the reservation, brilliant white and smooth against the bright blue Arizona sky. A classic Western Roman Catholic mission, Saint Xavier bore the cultural and architectural influence of Spain, Mexico and the Western Indians. The sanctuary was dark and cool, filled with ornate statues of the Virgin Mary (and other saints), candles, flowers and crumbling stucco. There was a damp and sweet smell — piety and poverty, I thought.

Next to the sanctuary was a small semi-open chapel, with candles burning and pictures of young Indian soldiers on the altar. Notes were attached to the pictures, "Please pray for my son in the Persian Gulf." Just outside the chapel a lovely, shy Indian girl sold chocolate bars to raise money for the mission. Buying two, I wanted to buy them all. I wanted to find some way to not feel the immense helplessness of those surroundings.

So there I stood in the Arizona dust, with my taco and tears, overwhelmed by sadness and alienation that seemed beyond redemption. I walked with my taco toward a cluster of bushes where I had seen a hungry dog. There behind the bushes I found him, drinking from a mud puddle. Bending down, I reached my taco toward him, feeling embarrassed for him and for me. He hesitated for a moment, but hunger overcame caution and he snatched the food from my hand, and in one swallow it was gone and so was he. Like the young Indian girl selling candy, I wanted to gather him up and take care of him forever. Unable to fix the plight of either, I contented myself with the brush of the dog's teeth against my hand and the exchange of money and candy with the Indian girl.

There are some things in life that cannot be fixed. There are some alienations that cannot be overcome. But there are some moments and gestures, however small, that provide us with a moment of redemption, however fleeting. So it was for me with a nameless hungry dog and shy Indian girl in the bright Arizona sunshine.

RAISING HANK

It was a spring ago that he came. I would like to think that he sought us out, but I know better. Nature permits little choice. It was by accident that we found each other.

It was our friend's daughter who first heard him above the din of our laughter, as the four of us stood that evening by our front door. Together, we knelt down and there beneath the holly bush, almost hidden in the mulch, was a day-old perfectly featherless baby bird. We searched in vain for his nest, but even with flash-lights could find not a clue of his origin. We thought of leaving him in hopes that his parents would return. In the end, the prospect of a cat or the weather claiming him persuaded us to bring him inside for at least a more humane death.

Through the night, my wife and I pushed cat food down his throat with our fingers and tried to keep his body temperature high enough to sustain such rapid metabolism. Toward dawn we said goodbye, certain he would not survive the night, and we fell into an exhausted sleep.

Then morning came; where we expected to find a dead baby bird in a shoe box was instead a very hungry bird, beak wide open and screeching for food! Thus began a six-week relationship of profound intimacy with a wild and primitive creature. A relationship that would touch us deeply and ultimately break our hearts. Susan, who has such an affinity for wild creatures and they her, moved naturally into a parenting role. I lingered a half-step behind, observing, waiting for my next instructions. We moved him from the shoe box into a plastic candy canister and covered the opening with a pair of panty hose, from which he drew his first name, Hanes. As my respect deepened for his overwhelming instinct to live, I began to call him Hank. In retrospect, perhaps some unconscious play on hawk.

I did not know it then but soon was to learn that raising a baby bird to maturity is a full-time job. A dozen live worms a day were required! Dear friends brought us worms and we became a familiar fixture at bait shops. Feeding intervals are every hour for baby birds and they cannot feed themselves. Consequently, each morning Susan left for her office with Hank in his candy canister under one arm and the day's supply of worms under the other. In the evening they returned from the day's work. It was quite a sight!

Hank flourished under Susan's nurture. He grew feathers and stood on a perch! In a few weeks he was too big for his canister and so we purchased his third and final home, a small gerbil cage. As he began to explore the larger world, he hopped in and out of his cage. And then one evening as we watched, he suddenly flew across the room. He was as startled as we were! He did not know he could fly!

Flying enabled Hank to begin a most tender ritual. He would fly from his cage to Susan's neck and there hide in her hair and peek out and nibble her ear with his beak, as if to say, "Here I feel safe."

The world is of course not a safe place, particularly if you are a bird. You must eat constantly, avoid predators, migrate thousands of miles, and reproduce yourself for two or three springs. I wanted to make Hank a pet and stave off the coming pain. Susan knew how cruel that would be, to deprive him of all that it means to be a wild bird. In the end Susan's wisdom prevailed and we set about the work of making Hank independent from us.

A million years of evolutionary instinct were starting to slam into place with the precision of a clock. We had very little time left to teach him to feed himself and keep his distance from people and animals. If we kept him much longer, he would lose his natural fear and be too vulnerable to survive in the wild. Quickly and with great patience, Susan frustrated him enough that he angrily began to feed himself. With growing sadness, we handled him less.

I greeted the morning of his release with dread, not wanting to let go. We ate breakfast in silence and tears with Hank in his cage between us. The world felt in slow motion. We each held him one last time and placed a light kiss atop his fragile head. He was now a full six inches long and fully feathered. So different from a scant six weeks before.

We took him onto our patio in his cage and opened the door. The sky was as blue and crystal clear as any spring day of my life. Other birds flew by chirping and mating. Hank simply sat in his cage, unaware that it was now his time. Susan reached in and put him on top of his cage and still he did not go. "Was he deciding to stay?" I suddenly found myself wondering, hoping. Susan took him over to the fence and perched him there and walked away. Then in a gesture that broke my heart, Hank flew from the fence over to Susan's neck and began to hide in her hair. In an act of such pure unselfishness that I do not expect ever to witness again, Susan harshly said "Go" and took him back to the fence.

Blinded by my tears, I tried not to blink. I did not want to miss the exact moment that instinct overcame dependency and he took his leave from us forever. Poised on the fence, he took one last look back at Susan and then responding to the ancient call of his kind, he left the fence in a long left-hand arch against the clear blue sky. In that instant he was gone and I was stunned. We wandered the back yard, calling out his name. Susan stayed in the yard the rest of the day. I walked the yard that evening calling out "Hank."

For months afterwards we thought perhaps we saw him in a tree here or there. While jogging I would call out "Hank!" to passing birds. In the weeks that followed, several friends reported unusually friendly birds at their houses and they wondered. Such was the magic!

It has been a year now and another spring is here. My tears come as easily as they did a spring ago. Tears of gratitude at the opportunity to briefly be a part of something so wild and mysterious. Gratitude at being present as a gulf between species momentarily closed. Gratitude at having my life dominated for six weeks by a bird. Gratitude for having things in my spirit touched that words cannot express.

A few mornings ago, I walked out into the front yard for the morning newspaper. The sky was as blue and crystal clear as was that other morning. A bird flew close by my head and the words were suddenly in my throat and heart. "Hank, I have not forgotten." As I turned toward the house, from a place somewhere else in my heart came T. S. Elliot's words:

> In the juvenescence of the year,
> In the springtime - at Easter
> Comes Christ The Tiger.

MY ATONEMENT

On my kitchen wall at home is a picture drawn by a 10-year-old girl. It is held in place by a colorful hot air balloon magnet. The picture is drawn with crayons on light blue lined school paper. The scene is of the 10-year-old in shorts and long flowing black hair, holding a leash on our large tan greyhound named Josh. Remarkable about the picture is how distinct and joyous Josh appears. One ear is up and he has a big dog smile on his face. In the upper left hand corner of the picture is a large yellow sun with several clouds floating across the sky. In the grass are a few streaks of yellow. It is a picture of a happy and carefree moment between a little girl and a grateful dog

The little girl came to live in our neighborhood a year ago with her mother, grandmother and sisters. It was not long before she wanted to meet our three greyhounds as we walked them past her house. Soon my wife was letting Toyne hold Josh's leash on the walks. Josh has a particularly sweet and gentle disposition that seemed to fit Toyne well. The picture in my kitchen is Toyne's expression of what it was like to hold Josh on the leash. The picture is large and full of color, seemingly expressive of joy and hope in new-found relationships.

As the year progressed, other people came and went at Toyne's house, some staying for several weeks or months. Toyne and her sisters were less often in the yard when we took our dogs for walks and Toyne walked Josh less often. Then one morning there was a great deal of commotion at Toyne's house. Apparently a car was being repossessed and in the process the car rolled into the side of the house, causing substantial enough damage that Toyne and her family had to move out.

All of this took place during a busy time of my life when I was often out of town. When I was home I was so hungry for private time that I made little attempt to connect with neighbors, especially Toyne and her family. Nor did I ask if I could help in some way after the car rolled into the house and they had to move. I assume that I justified my inaction with the thought that I was already helping many others and didn't have the energy or time for one more.

I do not now have a clear memory of when Toyne moved. Perhaps I was out of town trying to help someone do something. Whatever it was, it is no longer important enough to me to remember. But I do remember Toyne and what I did not do.

I never saw Toyne again, but her picture of a little girl full of hope with a new-found friend haunts me. I sometimes look at Josh and wonder if he remembers, and I sometimes look at the picture and wonder if Toyne remembers. My atonement ... is to remember.

NACHOS WITH MY MENTOR

I first met Bill Oglesby 23 years ago in Miami. I was two years out of seminary and in my first full-time parish appointment. Several of us had come together to organize a continuing education institute for clergy in South Florida. Bill was our invited speaker on marriage and family counseling. I not only had never heard of Bill, but as one of the officers of the institute, I even argued modestly for inviting someone with more name recognition!

Fortunately wiser heads prevailed. The evening before Bill's presentation I attended a small gathering in the apartment of a Catholic priest. There I was introduced to Bill. One who, as Bill was fond of quoting, "knew not Joseph." My memory two decades later is of being charmed and put at ease by Bill's wit, accent and gregariousness. He laughed much and loudly and enjoyed others and himself that evening. He must have told a dozen jokes between the rounds of nachos and the hottest jalapeno peppers we could find. He seemed equally to relish food and people, and I remember thinking what a large appetite for life he seemed to have. But what I most remember from that evening is Bill getting up from our festivities, going over to the phone, dialing a number and then, in a most uninhibited voice, singing happy birthday to his adult daughter! I have thought often of that moment and how loved his daughter must have felt by that single caring act.

The turnout the next day was large and enthusiastic.

Bill was engaging, funny and tender, and he spoke deeply to the needs of the clergy present. Then he was gone as quickly as he came and our paths did not cross again for some time.

Four years after that evening in Miami, I came to the Virginia Institute of Pastoral Care to learn pastoral counseling. I had not made the conscious connection and was thus surprised to learn that Bill had been one of the founders of VIPCare. For a long time I did not see much of him. He was busy teaching at Union Theological Seminary and when he was not, he was on the road speaking. He almost never turned down an invitation, believing that if he was invited, then the Lord must want him there for some reason. His Presbyterian heritage of predestination and providence helped foster that approach as did his love of travel and people.

What I do remember is that when Bill was present for VIPCare meetings, he was very present and involved and did not seem preoccupied by his other commitments. I was to learn from him much later that the schedule he maintained was not without its physical and emotional toll. But he used even that in his teaching of pastoral care and counseling.

I was fortunate to have Bill as a supervisor of my counseling work, though it was intimidating. Bill was fond of saying that the trouble with most people was that no one had ever cared enough to tell them the truth about themselves. In the first counseling case I ever presented, Bill began by correcting my grammar and went from there! He could tell the most truth with the most love of anyone I have known. Once when I had appeared before a membership committee and did not pass, Bill said, "Well, you went up and you came down!"

When Bill retired from the seminary he began to be

around VIPCare more frequently. Then six years ago VIPCare's board of directors asked Bill to become the interim executive director. At age 72 Bill did what he always did when presented with an invitation. He said "Yes" assuming the Lord had some reason.

Bill saying yes to that invitation generated a six-year friendship between the two of us that I shall hold dear the rest of my life. We worked closely together almost on a daily basis for a year, making some difficult decisions. If there was a decision to be made, Bill would go down the street to find it. If there was a bullet to be bitten, Bill would locate it before it was ever loaded in the gun. His energy at 72 was remarkable!

Our last five years consisted of an hour a week of what we loosely called consultation, but what we welcomed as an excuse to be together and tell stories about our lives and adventures, our joys and sorrows. While we never said it, I think we were preparing for Bill to leave and for me to go on without him. We were rehearsing.

At one of those meetings about a year ago, Bill poignantly noticed that his signature on my membership certificate was fading. In a silent and well-understood moment between us, I took the certificate out of the frame and Bill traced over his signature one final time.

The last time I saw Bill was three days before his death. We were conducting a series of video-taped conversations about his life. He stopped at my office door that Friday morning to remind me that we needed to get on each other's calendar to finish the project. We agreed on a date and wrote it in our books. I do not remember our final words. What I do remember is Bill's wife asking me on the day of his death if we had finished the taping. When I said no, Jan patted my hand and said,

"Well, you will have to finish alone." And so I will, I thought, as each of us does.

Yesterday was the six-month anniversary of Bill's death. I walked past Robert E. Lee's residence, which until a year ago had housed Bill's favorite restaurant, named for Lee's horse, Traveller. As I passed the residence, warm memories of a wonderful evening spent in the restaurant with Bill and Jan and my wife and daughter returned. My daughter was visiting and I wanted her to know this man who unashamedly sang happy birthday to his daughter in my presence 23 years ago. Bill was as utterly charming and engaging of Kristin that evening as he was of her father years ago in Miami.

It was my wife who captured my loss the day of Bill's funeral. As we walked under the large oaks toward the church, to no one in particular Susan said softly, "The whole world should grieve the passing of such a gentle soul."

WE SAY GOODBYE TO WHAT WE MUST

For well over a decade, one of my daily routines has been to run for a half hour at the end of my work day. The run has served as an antidote for the stress of the day's work and as a transition between work and home. I return relaxed and clear-headed and more human.

Until this fall, I have run mostly oblivious to things around me, usually absorbed in my own thoughts. But this fall has been different. When it first happened, I was startled by my response. Something caught my eye as I passed by. I ran a few steps more and then found myself returning to the spot. It was an automatic, instinctive response.

There in the grass lay a dead bird, a robin I remember. I felt overwhelming tenderness for this fragile friend and that his final resting place should not be in the grass beside a busy road. Feeling self-conscious of people passing by, I nonetheless picked up the robin, took him to a nearly bush and there laid him to rest beneath the early leaves of fall. In a ritual of sorts, I thanked this tiny winged creature for gracing the sky, said goodbye and returned to my run.

Since that encounter, I have been unable to pass a single dead bird without stopping to bury it. Now deep into fall, I have said many quiet and tender goodbyes beneath bushes.

Why after all these years of running and never seeing dead birds do I now have eyes to see? Perhaps as I move toward the fall of my own life, I am more aware of what this season brings, with its retreat into a dormancy that looks like death. Perhaps the shorter days and longer nights are reminders of the limits of life. Certainly the death of my colleague of 17 years, Bill Johnson, is a stark reminder that this life that we so love comes to an end.

Whatever the reason, I am grateful to have come upon this ritual of kneeling beneath bushes with lifeless birds. It is helping me to come to terms with the limits of life and it is connecting me to creatures great and small.

So in a season when I have laid to rest a beloved colleague and learned to bury dead birds, at my house we have adopted a manatee named Lucille and bought a hamster named Boomer. There is no separating life from death! We say goodbye to what we must while we love what we can.

KISSING LIFE ON THE MOUTH

Standing at the open door of the airplane looking down on the earth 11,000 feet below, I could only vaguely remember why I was getting ready to step out into space. The call had come to my hotel room in Milwaukee a few weeks before. It was my wife's voice, "What does your schedule look like on the 14th?" she asked. "It looks clear," I said in famous last words. "Good," she said, "I hope you were serious about wanting to leave a perfectly good airplane at 11,000 feet. I have arranged a sky dive for your 50th birthday!"

It was my own fault. I had been preoccupied with the idea of sky diving for well over a year. It seemed to me it would be one of those life events that would forever alter how one viewed and experienced life. I was also interested in what enables us to make deep level changes in our lives, the kind of change that requires trust in the unknown. In addition and more basically, I wanted to know how I would manage my fear and disorientation. The experience revealed all of those things and more.

By the time the six hours of ground instruction was over, I was overwhelmed by all there was to remember, especially the things to do if there were problems. By the time I climbed aboard the very noisy plane, I was becoming numb and disoriented from the sensory overload. Standing in the open door of the plane as we circled the jump site, I remember for a moment thinking that I could choose not to do this. And then as quickly, I let go of the plane and fell headfirst into space with a vague apprehension that it might be my last conscious act. Then there was only the sensation of cold air, noisily rushing by at 120 miles an hour, and the exhilaration of seeming to float in space.

The terror, the disorientation, the challenge was not in the fall through space, but in letting go of the security of the airplane. No skills or resources I had developed in 50 years of living prepared me to step out of an airplane at 11,000 feet. All I had to draw upon was six hours of instruction, a vague sense of trust, and a desire to see how I would manage my fear in the face of the unknown. Only later did I understand that I was needing to face my own death and that the sky dive was the vehicle I chose.

Not long after that birthday dive, I was in Chicago to teach a seminar. As I was writing some information on the blackboard that first morning, a voice from behind me in a soft drawl said, "I wanted you to know that my 14-year-old son was killed two weeks ago. I didn't know what else to do but come ahead to the seminar." In the week that followed, the owner of that voice blessed all of us as he allowed us to struggle with him in facing his terror and the unknown of that kind of loss. More than I, he knew what it meant to let go of security.

The night I returned from the seminar, there was a phone message that my wife's cousin and childhood playmate and my high school football teammate was dead of cancer, one year shy of seeing his 50th year of life. We had spent a few hours with him earlier in the year and I remember that he had that faraway look in his eyes of one already in the process of leaving. He and I spoke, but it was across the gulf of 32 years and we could only faintly hear each other or remember those robust days of courage on the playing field. Those memories as well as his life were slipping. I made little attempt to engage him and was content with respectful silence. I drove to our old practice field and remembered there our days of youth when our futures seemed to stretch unlimited before us. Our last words were as we shook hands in his front yard that night. I told him how beautiful and peaceful it seemed where he lived. We looked up at the bright stars against the clear South Florida sky and he said, "That's why I love it here."

Months later as my wife and I grieved over the phone message, she said amidst our tears, "As children, Ernie and I never, ever thought about dying. We just kissed and played." And so it is for most of us. We do not think much about our deaths or the deaths of those we love. Yet death is that which we have most in common with one another. This precious life that we come to so love does come to an end. The fact that it does makes the living of our days even more precious. It was to be reminded of that fact, I realized in retrospect, that led me to leave the security of an airplane at 11,000 feet on my 50th year of life.

It was an opportunity to face the inevitability of my own death and also, in the words of a friend, to kiss life on the mouth!

BEFORE THE ALTAR OF LOSS

I had been expecting the call. It was my younger daughter's voice, "Dad, Popper died last night." "I'm sorry, sweetie," I remember saying. Then silence as my 21-year-old struggled to find the words to wrap around the loss of her grandfather. "I think I would like to come down for the service," I said. "Let me call your mom and see if there is any problem with that," having long ago discovered how complicated simple acts can be for ex-spouses. But she was lovely and said, "Of course, your daughters will need you." And they would. But I was also aware of my own need to grieve and say goodbye to a father-in-law who had been in my life longer than my own father.

I was 14 and he was 43 when our 35-year relationship began. A high school romance between his daughter and me led to marriage and in-law status. In those years he was a gruff and intimidating man. But the death of his beloved wife turned him into a far more gentle person, though he never lost his general irritation with life.

When the great grief of the divorce between his daughter and me came, I was deeply touched that he chose to continue our relationship. In our 18 years as ex-in-laws (or whatever the term should be), he was more than cordial in my visits to see his granddaughters. What bitterness he may have had went unspoken in my presence. And for at least that kindness, I wanted to be there to say my thanks.

When the alarm clock woke me from a short and troubled sleep, it was still dark. A dawn flight took me the thousand miles to say my goodbyes. We gathered at his daughter's house for the drive to the church. We held our loss at bay with greetings, catching up, and food and drink.

Eventually we made our way to the church and gathered ourselves on one long front pew. We were spouses and ex-spouses, in-laws and ex-in-laws, boyfriends and ex-boyfriends. I think Popper would have loved the mix!

We seemed on that row a bit nervous and self-conscious as the service began. I opened my bulletin and it read, "A Service of Death and Resurrection for Cameron C. Booker." On the altar were two pictures. The first I recognized immediately. It was a formal and happy picture of Cameron and his wife, Mary, which Cameron kept displayed in his house across the 20-plus years since her death. A kind of memorial to their relationship, frozen in time. The other picture was of a more recent event. It was a casual picture of a relaxed and smiling Cameron at the railing of a cruise ship, with a drink in one hand and his pipe in the other. How content he looked and how pleased Mary would have been, I thought.

As from a distance, I became aware of the minister's voice as he read a lovely recollection by Cameron's daughter of the first song Cameron had taught her to sing, "Swing Low, Sweet Chariot." That was followed by a reading from "The Velveteen Rabbit," which spoke eloquently of Cameron's mellowing and becoming "real." As I listened, I felt the loss settling in and my grief arriving. As the choir began to softly sing "Swing Low, Sweet Chariot," I realized that all of us on that uneasy pew were united by the salt of our tears and made one by our loss. I handed my daughter my handkerchief and rested my hand lightly on her back. My tears flowed freely and felt holy before the altar of loss.

After the services, I came upon my older daughter's husband. I put my arms around him and said, "I know it is a loss for you, too." "He was like a father to me," he said, turning away so that I would not see his tears. He seemed especially alone with his grief and I felt especially helpless.

Finally, in one of those moments I would never have predicted, I stood alone in the church yard with my ex-wife's husband. "Thank you for coming all this way," he said. "I loved him," I replied. Without hesitation, we put our arms around each other and stood speaking of final things about this man we shared as a father-in-law. United in our loss, our barriers were at least momentarily transcended by Cameron's death.

The next night I sat in Cameron's dining room with my younger daughter and her boyfriend. In a precious gesture I will never forget, they fixed me a last dinner in Cameron's house. We spoke of many things. We laughed at his taste in decorating. I thought I would miss the smell of his pipe. My daughter wondered whom she would sit with in church. In a final gesture, we lifted our glasses in one last toast, "To Popper's life and spirit. We will love you and miss you forever." Then we gently touched our fragile glasses in the fading light of Cameron's house, surrounded by his precious memories.

GENUINE RECONCILIATIONS

For two decades I have had the privilege and pain of sitting with couples during difficult times in their relationship. Of the variety of reasons that bring couples to counseling, infidelity is one of the most painful and severest changes to the durability of a relationship.

Over the years I've tried to discern what enables some couples to survive infidelity and in some instances even deepen their relationship. It seems to be helpful if the couple has been together for a number of years and has weathered the variety of storms that life brings without an undue amount of chronic or intense conflict. It also seems helpful if the couple has a network of friends and relatives who are supportive of their relationship. And it seems helpful if the couple has a solid belief that there is a power beyond themselves that will see them through this painful time, regardless of the outcome. When those ingredients are present, there is a great possibility the couple may be able to undertake the hard work of reconciliation.

A number of things must happen for genuine reconciliation to occur and they are dependent on the couple spending many painful hours in conversation, often in the presence of a counselor. It is necessary for the offending partner to come to an understanding of the depth of hurt and betrayal experienced by his or her partner. Only through many hours of tears and anger can the offending partner begin to grasp the full impact of the infidelity on the relationship. Only then is the offending partner prepared to genuinely apologize, ask for forgiveness and consider what atonement may be necessary. And only then is the offended partner in a place to consider forgiveness.

For genuine reconciliation to occur, the couple needs to come to some understanding of the meaning of the infidelity in the context of their relationship. Was there anything about the nature of their relationship that contributed to the infidelity? And if they are people of faith they need to come to some understanding of the infidelity in the context of their relationship with God. What confession, atonement and forgiveness related to God are needed?

Some couples survive infidelity, some do not. Some who do stay together do not genuinely reconcile. Some couples do genuinely reconcile and deepen their relationship. What William Styron wrote regarding depression can be said of those couples who genuinely reconcile after infidelity has occurred, "For those who have dealt in depression's dark wood and know its inexplicable agony, their return from the abyss is not unlike the ascent of the poet, trudging upward and upward out of hell's black depths and at last emerging into what he saw as 'the shining world'. There, whoever has been restored to health has almost always been restored to the capacity of serenity and joy, and this may be indemnity enough for having endured the despair beyond despair."

ALTERING TIME IN TAMPA

On balance we all have a great capacity for accepting life as it is. Better than most other species, it seems to me. Having once accepted our lot in life, it is often only by accident that we notice that our arrangement with life has been changed. My cue was suddenly finding myself in an airport restroom face to face with a very startled woman and her daughter. Equally startled, I mumbled an apology and made a quick exit. As I did, a man who was obviously waiting outside for his wife and daughter, smiled and pointed me to the men's room. Embarrassed and trying to regain my composure, I managed to find the correct door. Upon entering, I heard the man say to his wife and daughter, "I guess it was more interesting on your side." And they were laughing as they walked away!

Once on the plane and relieved that the woman and daughter were nowhere in sight, much less seat mates, I began to explore why I had not paid more attention to where I was going. In the isolation of my seat at 30,000 feet, I began to understand the reason for my distraction. For the first time in the 15 years I had been flying between my daughters' home and mine, my older daughter was at the airport to say goodbye. It was the end of a weekend together in which the two of us had come home to each other after six years of estrangement.

In retrospect, like all retrospect, I should have seen the change coming. When I arrived that week, there was another first. Both of my daughters were at the airport to meet me. We laughed and hugged, and I told them how less lonely it felt to see them instead of the car rental agent.

The week's visit progressed uneventfully enough, until it came time to drive across state to Tampa for a workshop. My 19-year-old daughter who loves those kinds of trips asked if I minded if she didn't go. My older daughter, who had avoided being alone with me, announced that she planned to go instead.

For the first time in six years Heather and I found ourselves alone with each other for three days. We were tentative at first, but gradually began to relax. We broke the ice by stopping for a spring training game between the Astros and the Reds, where I discovered to my amazement that she loved baseball! It was the first of several things I was to discover. We spent the evenings in the hotel gym, followed by late and leisurely dinners that allowed us to gradually get to know each other again, but this time as adults. We talked enthusiastically about everything. Everything that is except the pain there had been when she had run away from home six years before. That we could not bring ourselves to touch, but what we were having seemed more than enough.

On our last day, I found myself slowly packing and watching the setting sun turn Tampa Bay a gorgeous flamingo pink. It was breathtaking and I was over-whelmed by sadness. From behind me I heard Heather ask, "What time do we need to leave, Dad?" When I turned to answer, she was sitting on the edge of the bed. For a moment time altered itself and I saw not the 23-year-old before me, but the 7-year-old who sat looking at her father in another time and place that had its own wounding.

Without realizing how I got there, I found myself on

my knees before her. The honest answer to that question came, "The truth is that I don't want to ever leave here. I don't want to give you up ever again." Tears began to run down her cheeks as she said, "Dad, I felt too guilty about the pain I know I caused all of you, to talk about it." By then she was on her knees and we were holding each other and sobbing. For the next hour as the Tampa sky went from pink to dark blue, the two of us sat on the hotel room floor, crying and holding each other and eventually talking and laughing. When we finally stood to finish packing, we both agreed it felt as if a great weight had been lifted from us.

The three-hour drive back home gave us time to talk about our mutual sojourns in the far country. Heather shared why she left, the details of her time on the road, how she had hugged her cat and blown a kiss to her sister the night she left. I shared with her my anguish and what I knew of her sister's pain, which had found expression in a high school essay, "I thought the silence that she left me with would explode inside of me." As we drove through the darkness, we acknowledged other painful things, but it was the kind of acknowledgment of pain that brings healing and closeness.

Finally, we were at Heather's doorstep and I delivered her back to husband and child. We hugged and she said she would see me in the morning at the airport. It was late, but I called Kristin for coffee. I wanted her to know what had happened between her sister and me. I wanted to tell her I deeply appreciated her wisdom and gift in deciding to not make the trip. In doing so she had purposefully created space for a reunion to occur. As I shared with her what had happened, her stoic eyes brimmed with tears and we had a long and tender embrace. I thanked her again for her gift of absence and we agreed that she and her sister needed a similar reunion.

At the airport the next morning, there was Heather! It had not been a mirage or an anomaly. Life does change and we change with it, back and forth. What life brings us I suppose is mostly a matter of timing and our openness to that timing.

I said to Heather as we held each other looking out on Tampa Bay that I would never forget that day, that hour, that hotel, that view of the bay as the sun set. I will forever hold that moment in a place precious in my heart, as a witness to the capacity of a daughter and a father to come home to each other. The moment was worth all the pain and all the waiting. It was enough.

PASSIVITY AND TELEPHONE POLES

I have rarely sought things in my life. For the most part, I have instead responded to that which has crossed my path. I believe my basic life stance in that regard began at an early near-death burn experience. I came so close to dying the first year of my life that I took a kind of comfort and refuge in a deep and internal retreat within myself. While I have no memory, save cellular, I sometimes imagine that in those weeks immediately after my burn experience I had to struggle to let go of death's hold on me in order to answer the call of life.

A profound and early childhood memory is of sitting in the back of my parents' car on long cross-country trips, watching the telephone poles go by and feeling a deep and comfortable passivity. Not unlike what I imagined my internal state to have been in those weeks that I hung between life and death.

A prevailing memory of elementary school is of feeling painfully self-conscious and shy, feelings that I still have these five decades later whenever I enter a roomful of people. I have come to understand that my feelings of acute self-awareness, self-doubt and insecurity also have their origin in my burn experience.

Harry Stack Sullivan is reported to have said that by the time he figured out why he had become a psychiatrist it was too late! Certainly that is true for all of us. Each of us is shaped by the variety of traumatic and not so traumatic events that have occurred in our lives. All of the moments and people, good and bad, have gone into making us who we are and influencing our choices in life.

Those personality characteristics of mine that issued out of the trauma of my burn experience, while limiting me in certain ways, have also been gifts. My self-consciousness has helped me to be more aware of myself and others than I may otherwise have been. My shyness has helped me to be comfortable with being alone. So much so that I have had wonderful sightseeing experiences by myself in a great variety of places I have traveled. Even my self-doubt has been useful. I believe it has saved me, at least some of the time, from arrogance. And, it has caused me to be doubly careful when making decisions.

The passivity I remember as a child in the back seat of my parents' car has matured into an individuation and disengagement. By that I mean that I am not particularly reactive to my world and feel comfortable in many different situations. Because of that early passivity, it is easy for me to enter into situations, but it is also easy for me to let go. A few things matter a great deal to me, but many things do not.

These dynamics have brought me to a way of doing my life that I have come to think of as answering a succession of spiritual calls. I somewhat jokingly say that I do not volunteer for anything, but I say yes to almost everything asked of me within reason. It is the truth of how I have come to live my life as calling. That basic prescription has kept me from wanting and seeking things out of my own ego and has led me into wonderful and challenging situations and experiences that I would never have have chosen on my own.

Along the way I have been blessed by the love and encouragement of wonderful people. That love and encouragement have enabled me to embrace my limitations and to even see my near-death experience as a gift! Thus, I am content to refrain from seeking and instead to respond to that which crosses my path. My experience is that as I do that, I am more likely to meet God along the way.

THEREIN TO BE CONTENT

For some time now I have been realizing the obvious. In general, we either do not get our first choice in life, or our first choice, when we do get it, does not work out as well as second choice. There are exceptions to be sure, but I am gradually coming to accept this as a basic life truth.

In an era when first choices are often easier to come by than ever before, this may seem a silly thought. Yet in spite of the constant if not chronic societal admonition of "go for the gusto," many of our first choices do not bring us contentment. It is not that they are wrong choices, it is more that first choices often turn out to not offer as much as they initially seem to offer.

Some second marriages and blended families turn out to be richer than the first. The line, "Love is lovelier the second time around," attempts to set forth that notion. Of course, second choice is not always better and second choice is almost always painful. But sometimes second choice is better for us. Some adopted families are better than the family of origin. Sometimes not being admitted to a particular school or not getting a particular job leads one in a totally different direction from the one that would have been taken if first chosen. While disappointing, second choice may ultimately be better.

When we look at life closely, perhaps the majority of life is filled with second choices. Whether we are content or even happy with second choice depends largely on our attitude. That is, whether we are able to turn loose our white-knuckled grip on having to have our first choice and turn our energy to second choice. It is the truism behind the rather trite "when life gives you lemons, make lemonade." Much of the pain of life has to do with having too much energy invested in first choices that have not worked out. Conversely, much of what is involved in seeking health has to do with letting go of first choices we did not get or that did not work and investing ourselves in second and sometimes even third choices. Much of the healing of the wounds of our past depends on letting go of the past and embracing what today offers.

My father, dead for 25 years, was my first choice. But because of his past and what he was not able to let go of, he was unable to be the kind of father I needed. Instead, my grandfather, who was my second choice, became the father that I needed.

When my grandfather died four months into his 91st year, I said of him at his funeral, "I have never known a man who knew so well how to live, or how to die. He slipped imperceptibly from us during this past year with the same grace and gentleness that so character-ized his life, as if to ease us to this final loss. I told a friend that I was afraid I would feel terribly alone and empty when granddaddy was gone, because he had given me so much. My friend said, 'Surely you are overlooking your grandfather's gift — that what he has given you will never go away. You will carry what he has meant inside yourself always, even after he is gone.' My friend was right. Who granddaddy was will con-tinue on within each of us, and in that sense he does not leave us. This good man has taught us so much about living, gentleness, compassion, integrity, music, humor, and how to love. At his 90th birthday, four months ago, having learned in his blindness with Paul, 'in whatsoever state I am, therein to be content,' this remarkable man stood and greeted each person who arrived, kissed the women, blew out every candle on his cake, and told two very funny jokes! How much he loved living and how very well he lived! So we grieve not for granddaddy, but for ourselves. But we do not grieve as those who have no hope, for we are persuaded with the Apostle Paul, 'that neither life, nor death, nor anything else in all creation, shall be able to separate us from the love of God.' Nor shall death separate us from this good man. Husband, father, grandfather, great-grandfather, brother, friend — we love you. We will miss you forever. So until the time comes to be with him in that great house God has prepared, we give thanks for him who brought life and immortality to light. Well done thou good and faithful servant!"

A second choice, without which my life would have been greatly diminished. A second choice for which I will always be grateful!

THE TIDE OF TIME

I write this four days removed from performing my daughter's wedding. A unique benefit of being both a father and a minister! Since my mind has had little room for anything else except wedding plans, I share with you some of the remarks I made at the rehearsal dinner, the wedding ceremony and reception. All invited by my daughter Kristin and son-in-law John!

At the rehearsal dinner I offered the following toast, "A quote that has been particularly meaningful to Kristin and John has been this one from the movie Forces of Nature, 'Marriage has less beauty but more safety than the single life. It is full of sorrows and full of joys. It lies under more burdens, but it is supported by all the strengths of love. And those burdens are delightful.' This time tomorrow, Kristin and John will no longer have the single life. They will have the sorrows and joys of marriage that is supported by all the strengths of love. Delightful burdens! Tonight, on the eve of their marriage, we pause to reflect on the journey that has brought these two separate lives together and to marvel at the mystery of how time and events cause unrelated lives to intersect in such a way that the rest of their lives are inextricably bound together forever. A colleague shared these words, 'Fine wine takes time, patience and special soils and containers which allow the fruit to reach its fullest potential. Then, when moments are right, we sit back and take in the great flavors that flow from this process. Not unlike our journey with children.' Tonight, the moment is right for taking in the great flavors, Kristin and John - we love dearly and take joy in your marriage!"

During the wedding ceremony, I shared the following reflections in response to a variety of readings. "In the very best of marriages, there develops a growing capacity to stand closer and closer to one's partner, while maintaining one's own distinctness. Healthy, mature couples neither have to withdraw in emotional distance, nor fuse and lose their own identity. Marriage has enormous power to bring pain and joy. It is a container within which two people can grow through the influence of the other, or have their very selves diminished because of the other. Marriage can build each partner up, or it can tear each partner down. For a marriage to be successful, it requires of each partner a capacity for openness and flexibility and a capacity to tolerate the anxiety of being known so intimately by another. Only marriage teaches us how to be married! No books or speeches can do that. You don't work on your marriage — your marriage works on you. It takes you to places you never expected to go, both pleasant and unpleasant. The task of marriage is to see the journey as creative, even redemptive. An opportunity to become a deeper and richer person than you ever would have been without your partner."

At the reception I offered a final toast. "In the New Testament is this elegant line, 'Since we are surrounded by so great a cloud of witnesses...' We are surrounded at these tables by pictures of Kristin and John and their family members. Pictures taken over the course of three decades, in all times and circumstances. Some of those in the pictures are here and there are others whose love yet endures from afar. Truly a great cloud of witnesses! Better than I, Frederick Buechner says, 'The tide that carries us farther and farther away from our beginning in time is also the tide that turns and carries us back again… I believe that what we long for most in the home we knew is the peace and charity that, if we were lucky, we first came to experience there, and I believe that it is that same peace and charity we dream of finding once again in the home that the tide of time draws us toward.' The tide of time has drawn Kristin and John to one another and to their own home where peace and charity can be known. We toast them and send them on their way with yet another elegant New Testament line, 'Be watchful and firm in your faith, be courageous, be strong. Let all that you do be done in love.'"

OUR PLACE OF CHARITY

Pat Conroy opens his elegant novel The Prince of Tides with, "My wound is geography. It is also my anchorage and port of call." Mine too! Locations and houses and rooms have always stirred me.

Recently on the Eastern Shore of Virginia, my family gathered to do the things necessary to prepare my grandparents' 250-year-old home to be sold. It was our second and what we thought would be final trip.

A year ago, after my grandmother's death at age 98, children and grandchildren and great-grandchildren gathered to remember and select tangible memories from the house. Among my prized possessions from that gathering are the walnut desk at which my grandfather sat and paid bills and the very worn knife my grandmother used to open clams behind the mill.

As a child, summer after summer in that place, I was surrounded by well-told stories, much laughter and the smell of seafood cooking. In that place, on that land, in that house, in those particular rooms, I came gradually to experience the certainty that I was loved and that life could be trusted. It was such a gorgeous gift that I have fed from it all the rest of my life. To whatever degree as an adult I have been able to love and care for others, it is because of what I received all those summers as a child in that dear place from those dear people who told stories around the dinner table and laughed much.

More profoundly than I, Frederick Buechner says in The Longing for Home, "The tide that carries us farther and farther away from our beginning in time is also the tide that turns and carries us back again. In other words, it is true what they say: The older we grow, the more we find ourselves returning to the days when we were young. More vividly than ever before, I think, we find ourselves remembering the one particular house that was our childhood home. We remember the books we read there. We remember the people we love there. I believe that what we long for most in the home we knew is the peace and charity that, if we were lucky, we first came to experience there."

Thus, did my family gather recently at our place of charity, to remember. My wife ran the video camera as my uncle and mother and others remembered aloud for future generations. Once again, stories were well told amidst much laughter. New and simpler mementos were gathered. A walnut from beneath the walnut tree in the front yard. A clam shell from beside the branch. Yellowing pictures and letters from the floor of the mill. Excavations of a life and era.

Among the accidentally found pictures on the mill floor was one of me as a child with a dog named Sport. My grandfather often told the story and because he did, I came to understand that it meant something to him, though I never asked. He said that when Sport died, I went with him to bury Sport behind the mill. He said that when we were finished I took a clam shell and placed it on top of the grave. He said as we walked away, I looked back over my shoulder and said, "Goodbye, Old Sport."

If grief is love's struggle to let go, then that is what we were about as a family on the Eastern Shore. An attempt to say "goodbye old house, goodbye old mill, goodbye grandmother and granddaddy." Yet in the midst of our goodbyes and attempts to let go, we were also gathering and preserving and holding on.

One of the great-grandchildren at the gathering had just completed her master's thesis a year too late for her mother to see it. Kristin brought the bound green thesis to the gathering. Inside was an acknowledgment to her mother. It said, "To Darlene Hoibraten, for her unfailing belief in my abilities, and for her love, which endures from afar." The witness of a daughter who knows that all the love that we have ever received or given is not lost to time.

Twenty-five years after my father's death, he came to me in a dream so sublime that I wept. He was happy and he kissed me. I awoke certain of his kiss. It never happened again, but in all of the years since, I have been reassured that in the end we shall find and know again all those whom we have lost. Perhaps we shall even know the houses and rooms, the stories and laughter, and the smells of favorite foods cooking!

MORTGAGE AND MOM

My mother is amazing! Last month at the age of 78 she made the final payment on her 30-year mortgage. She made the last payment with the same quiet and unassuming grace with which she has made each of the 360 payments over the past three decades. She paid her mortgage by herself and insofar as I know without ever needing help or ever missing a payment.

As a young girl of 18 my mother left the security of her small community to marry a "come-here," as they were called. Because of that marriage she saw more of this country and learned more about the variety of people in this country than ever would have happened had she remained in her hometown. My father passing through Bloxom forever altered the course of her life.

As a young 23-year-old mother, she had to face the horror of the potential death of her 1-year-old child. As she describes that moment, she was heating grease to fry potatoes when her son pulled the pan of grease off the stove and onto himself. The burns were third degree. After the doctors at the hospital treated him, they told her that they did not think he would survive the trauma and that she might as well let him die at home. For the next several weeks my mother and father slept crossways in the bed with their only child between them. Crossways, so that they would be uncomfortable enough that they would not sleep too deeply.

The year was 1945. It was the week of the death of President Franklin Roosevelt. My mother remembers that the accounts of Roosevelt's death and funeral were the only things to be heard on the radio. There was constant sad music. Thus was my parents' grief compounded by the national grief, without even the radio to distract. That moment in their lives must have been suffocating and unrelenting in its intensity, as they waited on the death of their child.

Every few days this young mother would take her son to the hospital to have the bandages and dressing changed. So burned was her son she said, that people on the hospital elevator would cry when they got on. Then one day, the doctor said to my mother, "He is going to make it." Only then she said did she permit herself for the first time to cry. And only once decades later, sitting in an airplane seat beside her, did I see out of the corner of my eye, the tears in her eyes as we talked about that long ago moment of anguish. It was there, high above the country that my mother gave me an indescribable gift. Quietly, in her understated way, while looking straight ahead, she said, "Nothing else that came after that ever changed your place in my heart."

Time and events and decades passed. Another child, another husband and a life in Florida. Then another loss and at age 48, three decades after leaving, my mother returned to Virginia to begin a whole new life. She found a house to buy and continued to make payments on a house in Florida, all on the salary of a waitress and never once complaining!

Sometime during the last 30 years as she made those payments and I wasn't paying attention, she became a major baseball and football fan. On her 75th birthday, I surprised her with a trip to Florida to see the Atlanta Braves in spring training. We sat right behind home plate and she amazed me with her baseball knowledge. When I slipped away and asked the announcer to announce her name and birthday, she was most pleased with the recognition, but not equally pleased that he also mentioned her age! This month, in recognition of that 360th mortgage payment, instead of a mortgage burning, I will take her once again to Florida, this time to see her favorite football team play! It seems fitting for someone still so young.

My mother would have me tell you about her failures, insecurity and guilt. Never mind! Those things pale in comparison to her courage, work ethic, openness, sense of humor, tolerance and capacity to be content. She has, simply put, great character!

A colleague told me that at her seminary the school hired a renowned retired minister to teach preaching. Freshly returned from a trip to China, the first thing that 85-year-old Dr. Buttrick did when he arrived in Louisville was to take out a 30-year mortgage. What a wonderful capacity to face the future with hope and expectation. How wonderful it is to watch my mother do the same!

THE PLACE IN THE WOODS

If it is true that the apple does not fall far from the tree, then it is true that I am a nomad. How else could I have turned out? After all I was the child of a "fruit tramp," growing up in the back seat of my father's car as he followed produce crops across the country. There was Florida, Virginia, Texas and California, usually in the same year — back and forth across the country. So much was travel a part of my early life that in writing a grade school autobiography (which my mother still has), I described at length my most recent trip to California, including pictures!

In those travels I learned early and intuitively that home was whatever town and state I happened to be in and that all was well, so long as I was with my parents – and had food! The issue with food, as my mother tells it, is that I would not go into a motel until we first stopped and bought a snack to take in with us. An interesting symbol of security that remains with me to this day! Home was more a state of mind than place, though there were places that held significance and security for me — but they were not mine. Predictably, I chose or was chosen by an occupation that required frequent moves. Thus until my mid-thirties I lived nowhere longer than four years! Sigmund Freud's term was repetition compulsion, to recreate our family of origin experience in adulthood.

Then 20 years ago I moved into a house and moved no more. I remember feeling vaguely restless during the fourth year in that house. It was as if an unconscious alarm clock had gone off within me, alerting me that it was time to move again. But the feeling subsided with the passage of time, and I remained in that house.

As the years passed, my professional involvements afforded me the opportunity for increasing amounts of travel. More than once friends and colleagues commented on how easily I seem to travel and how home seems to be wherever I am. And if the truth be told, and I am trying, I am never happier than when I have an airline ticket in my pocket and am headed somewhere interesting. I am among a minority who still loves to fly, finds airports exciting, truck stops irresistible and who harbors a not-so-secret fantasy of driving an 18-wheeler coast to coast.

Because of my love of travel and early life experience, it has been hard for me to feel truly at home in my house. But six months ago, that changed. After 20 years in the same house, we moved into a cedar house that sits on a hill in the forest surrounded by plants and wildlife. In this place of beauty, where the indoors merges with the outdoors, I am reconnected to nature and have come home to myself. It is a transforming place and I am transformed by it! In that place of comfort, I am coming to realize that until now I never had a home, only places where I lived.

It is not that my love of travel has been diminished by this bright place that I now call home. In fact these words come while returning from the same California that I traveled to so many times in the back seat of my parents' car. A trip that took a week in those days will take me seven hours this day. It remains an old and familiar and comfortable feeling, this movement back and forth across the United States.

What is different is that on this trip I miss being at

home more keenly than I have ever missed any other place I have lived. I miss the welcoming feel of the house, the expansiveness of space, the sense of living in the midst of nature. This place in the woods has come to be my house of belonging. It is the place where I have come home to myself and where I have come in order to love all those things that it has taken me so long to learn to love.

PASSING THE TORCH

The black desk on the second floor of my home sits in front of a window that looks out onto the tops of trees that form dense woods. On that desk are three cards. One of the three is the card with the gold embossed seal that has taken me a thousand miles south, to a town I have been returning to for the past 25 years.

The town is a classic small south Florida town, 30 miles south of Cape Kennedy on the east coast of Florida. Melbourne sits on the inter-coastal waterway, two miles from the Atlantic Ocean. It is an old town and is populated by what used to be called "Florida Crackers," a term used to describe the fiercely independent characters who carved out a lifestyle of fishing, farming and cattle raising in what was then a relatively inhospitable environment.

By the 1960s there were a growing number of engineers and scientists working on the nearby space program and then a growing number of retirees, fleeing the snowy north for this quiet, sunny, riverside town. The cracker influence has mostly vanished, save for the old wooden houses and an occasional local bar with a sign that says, "Open at 8:00 a.m." The warm weather and casual life style have attracted a growing number of homeless. The town is now a mixture of old and young, rich and poor, educated and uneducated – all drawn to the sun and the water. It is this town that I moved from in 1976, and that as a part-time father I have returned to several times a year for the past 25 years. It is to this town that the gold embossed card brought me.

In the center of the card is a gold picture of the earth with a space vehicle in orbit around it and the inscription "Ad Astra Per Scientiam." Around the gold earth, in red, the seal reads "Florida Institute of Technology 1958." Inside is a drawing of a building with palm trees and in script, "Kristin Dawn Horishny, Doctor of Psychology, Clinical Psychology Specialization, Degrees will be awarded Saturday, September eighth, Two Thousand One At eleven o'clock in the morning, Gleason Auditorium, Melbourne, Florida."

My daughter! How could it be that my daughter could be addressed as "doctor"? It was only yesterday that I was getting used to the title for myself! I have long understood and even lectured about the inter-connectedness of the generations and what it means to pass the torch from generation to generation. But sitting in Gleason Auditorium beside Kristin's grandmother as Dr. Richard Elmore proudly placed the colorful academic hood over Kristin's head, I experienced for the first time what it means for the torch to be passed.

Surprised by how deeply moved I was, I thought back to the second card on my desk. It is a Father's Day card from a few years ago. The front of the card reads, "Do what you love, the rest will come." Inside the card Kristin wrote, "When I saw this card, I realized that following your heart, so to speak, is one of the most important things I have ever learned from you. You always taught me to believe in myself and to do what I love, and that if I did, everything else would be ok. Thank you for instilling in me such a remarkable way of life."

After the ceremony, Kristin's husband's family gathered with Kristin's family at a marina hotel with a balcony overlooking a wonderful variety of boats. There admidst many congratulations, gifts were opened including Kristin's great-grandmother's wristwatch. Toasts were made, including one in which I said, "There are those we love who are not with us any longer, including Kristin's mom Darlene and Kristin's dear friend Avis."

Kristin had worn to graduation a new bracelet with her mom's name on it as a way of remembering. As we left the auditorium a couple seated on a low wall caught my eye. I couldn't place them until I walked up and saw the tears in their eyes. It was Avis' parents. Kristin and Avis had been friends since elementary school. Avis had married and had children, later became seriously ill, and far outlived her prognosis. She died a few months before this graduation day. Avis' mom and I hugged several times, and all I could offer was to say, "I am so sorry..." As I walked away from them, I felt a sense of guilt that I had my daughter and they no longer had Avis.

There was another moment. The evening before graduation, Kristin presented me with a small blue photo album. The picture on the front is of a very tiny and very bald baby girl! Page by page reveals a succession of significant events in the life of this bald baby girl. Until coming to the final picture of the two of us last year in front of Gleason Auditorium when Kristin received an award as the outstanding clinical psychology student. The card with the album is of Pooh Bear writing a note, "Thank you for making me feel like a very important somebody! You shouldn't have...but I'm ever so glad you did." Inside Kristin wrote, "Thank you for helping to make the journey so remarkable. It is such a gift to be able to share so much with you. May the future hold equally wonderful moments!"

The third card on my desk overlooking the woods is

of a little girl sitting on a man's shoulders hugging the top of his head. The inscription, "Loved the view. Loved you. Still do. Happy Father's Day!"

A blessing, undeserved but transforming in its graciousness.

THE PURSUIT OF SPIRITUAL WHOLENESS

Several years ago I was in Sedona, Arizona. Sedona is beautiful red rock country north of Phoenix, where many of the John Wayne movies of the 50s were filmed. Sedona has become one of the special gathering places for New Agers. They consider it one of the three strongest energy vortexes in the world, according to a brochure I read in my hotel room. My wife Susan, who is not a New Ager, but who does like crystals, had asked me to bring her back something called a window crystal – which I discovered is a crystal within a crystal. Extra power – I think!

In hopes of getting a really good window crystal, I picked the largest crystal shop I could find, The Crystal Palace. A bright pink and glass building on the corner. There in The Crystal Palace, I found myself standing in line waiting to pay for the really good window crystal I found. In front of me was a woman in her early 30s with long brown, slightly uncombed hair, dressed in a peasant dress and sandals. She looked a bit disorganized and mildly distraught. Beside her was a lovely and matching little girl with long brown hair, peasant dress and sandals. As I stood behind them, the little girl tugged at her mother's dress and said, "Mommy, why are we buying that crystal?" To which the mother said, "Sweetie, Mommy is having trouble making contact with the archangel Michael and this will help."

While I kept quiet eavesdropping on their exchange, their conversation was a reminder to me of the kind of spiritual hunger there seems to be in our society and all the different non-traditional expressions it takes. Go in any bookstore in America and the shelves are full of books on spirituality, many of them non-traditional and non-religious. People are buying these books out of what seems to be a spiritual homelessness. Out of what seems to be a longing for meaning, transcendence and healing.

It is against this backdrop that I have been trying to understand what constitutes spiritual wholeness. It is a spirituality that is not self-centered, that is nurturing throughout one's life, and that calls one to love one's neighbor and to work for justice.

Wally Fletcher says that every person has four spiritual hungers, whether we recognize them or not. The first is a longing for a way to experience the deeper dimension of life. Sooner or later we develop a sense of frustration with superficiality, or of life not lived below the eyeballs! The purpose of spiritual wholeness, of religion, is to help to see below the surface of everyday existence and to reconnect with the depth dimension of life.

The second spiritual hunger is a longing for a way to experience centeredness. We spend much of our lives feeling fragmented and pulled in many directions. Our hunger is for groundedness. Or put another way, where we belong and to whom we belong!

A third spiritual hunger is a longing for a way to acknowledge our feelings of dependency in the universe. The biblical narrative reminds us that we are God's creations and ultimately that we belong to God. Or as Augustine put it, "Restless are our hearts until they rest in thee."

Our fourth spiritual hunger is a longing for a way to experience community and belonging. Our deep spiritual need is for intimacy, connection and community.

If those are our spiritual hungers, what then are ways to meet those hungers? In my opinion it is the pursuit of spiritual wholeness that can point us in the proper directions. So what are the characteristics of spiritual wholeness?

Flexibility and openness are two. All of the deeply religious people I have known, the ones I would consider saints alive, have had great openness and flexibility. They have had the capacity to take in and tolerate the new, and in essence to become all that they had the power to become as God's creation.

The spirit blows where it will, we are reminded by the Bible. Our task in the pursuit of spiritual wholeness is to be open to perceive the activity of the spirit as it occurs and not to have to make it conform to some preconceived mold that we hold. The idea has been put nowhere lovelier than in W. H. Anden's, "I know nothing except what everyone knows – if there when grace dances, I should dance!" And the antithesis nowhere better stated than in a colleague's comment that no amount of genius can overcome a preoccupation with detail! God is in us seeking creativity, which requires our openness and flexibility. But often our tendency is to seek safe harbor in that which is familiar and known.

I once heard the president of the Baptist seminary in Richmond say, "Nostalgia is the fear that God's activity has peaked somewhere in the past and all the faithful have left is to long for the good old days." Shrinking our world down to that within which we can feel safe is the opposite of being open and flexible.

Shortly before Wilbur and Orville Wright lifted off from Kitty Hawk, Lord Calvin announced that heavier than air vehicles cannot fly. After word came back to Dayton, Ohio (the hometown of Wilbur and Orville) that they had flown, the editor of the local newspaper wrote that it could not have happened, and if it did happen, it would not be anyone from Dayton! And in 1899, the head of the patent office announced that everything that can be invented had been invented!

Spiritual wholeness on the other hand has to do with expanding and enlarging our sense of self and world. Being alive in such a way that we allow ourselves to be created fresh, over and over is, I think, what the Bible means when it says that the Lord's mercies are new each morning.

So the pursuit of spiritual wholeness involves openness and flexibility, to which I would add attentiveness and expectancy. Jim Bugenthal has said, "The real voyage of discovery is not in some new landscape, but in having eyes!" A task of spiritual wholeness is to live as fully present and aware as possible with an expectancy of discovery. Unlike the cartoon I once saw of a family out walking and the little girl says, "Mommy, are we live or on tape?" Being on tape is living every day the same, without expectation of the new breaking in, without seeing what is around us. It is lip-syncing life. And habitual, repetitive patterns can deaden us to the wonders all around us.

Sallie McFague has written a wonderful book about attentiveness and expectancy. She writes that, "Most of the time we do not see; we pass a tree, an early Spring crocus, the face of another human being, and we do not marvel at these wonders, because we do not see their specialness, their individuality, their difference." She then says she has come to believe that absolute attention is a form of prayer. She suggests that by paying absolute attention to something we are, in fact, praying. She goes on to say, "Over the years I have learned that the closer attention I pay to whatever piece of the world is before me – the more I know about it, the more open I am to its presence, the closer I look at it or listen to it or touch it or smell it – the more amazed I am by it. It is the specialness, the difference, the intricacy of each creature, event, or aspect of nature, that calls forth wonder." That is as apt a description as any I know about what it means to be attentive and expectant! It is a reminder of Alice Walker's comment that she believes it upsets God if we pass by the color purple in a field and do not notice!

Openness, flexibility, attentiveness and expectancy. The marks of spiritual wholeness. Our invitation to spiritual wholeness is to peer deeply into the creation and into the hearts of those with whom we share this world, seeking there the image of God. Our invitation is to attend to the presence of God in our lives and the world around us and to assist others to attend to God's presence in their life and world.

This collection of vignettes has been an attempt to do just that.

THE VIRGINIA INSTITUTE
OF PASTORAL CARE

The Virginia Institute of Pastoral Care, familiarly known as VIPCare, was founded in 1967. Its founders saw the need to offer pastoral counseling to individuals outside a hospital setting and at a skill level generally beyond that of the local minister.

VIPCare is an interfaith, not-for-profit pastoral counseling and educational institute. Its counselors are ministers of various faiths and are certified by the American Association of Pastoral Counselors.

Individual, marital, family and group counseling are offered by VIPCare staff members, who bring a unique sensitivity to the dynamics of behavior and faith. VIPCare services are available to persons of all ages, races, genders, religious beliefs and cultures regardless of their ability to pay.

Many clients are seen at VIPCare's main office on Bremo Road in Richmond. Others are seen at satellite centers located at churches in Richmond, Ashland, Bon Air, Chester and Williamsburg.

Other programs offered by VIPCare include:

- Congregational Care, education for lay people chosen by their pastors and congregations to provide caring support.
- Pre-Marriage Seminars for couples engaged or recently married.
- Parish Pastoral Care, designed for parish ministers

and other church professionals who seek to increase skills in pastoral care.

- Conflict Management, Education and Consulting Services.
- Clinical Education in Pastoral Counseling.

In addition, presentations on a variety of topics are offered to congregations and community groups in Central Virginia by the VIPCare staff as an educational service.